SOON YOU'LL BE A
BIG CELEBRITY

LEWIS MANCINI, MD

Order this book online at www.trafford.com
or email orders@trafford.com

Most Trafford titles are also available at major online book retailers.

Print information available on the last page.

ISBN: 978-1-6987-1525-4 (sc)
ISBN: 978-1-6987-1526-1 (e)

Library of Congress Control Number: 2023915586

Trafford rev. 08/15/2023

 www.trafford.com

North America & international
toll-free: 844-688-6899 (USA & Canada)
fax: 812 355 4082

DEDICATION

This booklet is dedicated to
my late friend Herbert Bucki
and to my brother Douglas Taylor.

CONTENTS

INTRODUCTION

Soon You'll Be A Big Celebrity is a collection of essays that can be classified as scientific and religious speculation. Some of the material here may seem a little "far out," but as you read the essays you may begin to develop an alternate version of the future, of your future.

Some of this material has appeared in Lewis Mancini's previous writings (see *Appendix: Other Writings by Lewis Mancini*).

~Editor

P.S. Just because I would prefer a universe where everyone, including God, is equal doesn't make it so. However, it could become true in the future. If there is a God, she or he would know I would be lying if I didn't admit to my preference.

~LSM

"Soon You'll Be A Big Celebrity" is an essay which explains how it is that you're already a galactic celebrity but the finite universe is too jealous to let you know about your celebrity. It is also about the realization that when you die, you'll be informed that you've been famous all along. And after death you'll be able to enjoy your celebrity.

Our Galaxy is Our Finite Universe

A galaxy is a cluster of stars (i.e., suns) and planets which is separated from other galaxies by huge expanses of space. For the purpose of this essay <u>each galaxy</u> may be considered a <u>finite universe</u>. Some astrophysicists have conjectured that there are only a finite number of galaxies. But this does not make much sense.

It seems to me that space must be infinite and must go on forever. And there must be an infinite number of galaxies, each with its own God (president of the finite universe) who everyone in the galaxy gets a turn to be. If everyone gets a turn to be God or, synonymously, president of the galaxy/finite universe, then everyone is equal. This equality makes for a particularly stable finite universe, because there would be no rivalry and equality would be a given.

The reason why space is probably infinite is that if space comes to an end, then what lies beyond the "end"? A solid barrier of infinite thickness <u>or</u> more space. If it were a solid barrier or wall, what would it be made of? More empty space makes more sense.

Planet Earth is probably the central reference point of our Milky Way galaxy. This is because if there were any more suffering than what's here on Earth, the galaxy would be too unstable to exist. What's unique about Earth is suffering. Except for Earth, there is probably no suffering in our galaxy. All present, past and future earthlings (including non-human ones) have the unique property of suffering. There are at least four reasons why there must be some suffering. Each galaxy that is bigger than a certain size, must have some suffering at its central reference point.

WHY THERE MUST BE SOME SUFFERING

Each large galaxy contains one planet where there is suffering. This is hell and planet Earth is the hell of the Milky Way galaxy. Hell is the center stage central reference point for time and space. Without this central hell, heavenites wouldn't be able to cooperate their activities. Why only one hell per large galaxy? Small galaxies don't need a hell.

Every few thousand years, God says "And the next hell will be right here" and He points to the planet that will become the next center of the galaxy. And everyone, wanting to be center-stage famous, rushes to that hell-planet. But only a relatively small number of souls get to live there and only temporarily. Those souls who get closed out are so jealous that they will not cooperate with the finite universe/galaxy unless all science and technology are taken away from the center-stage souls who are forced to live in caves without technology. Gradually, the closed-out souls' jealousy/anger dies down and science and technology are restored to the hell-planet. This long process is what we know as "progress." The end-point of progress is full heavenization.

So the real sin is the greediness for fame. And this forces the existence of suffering. Jealousy and greed for fame cause suffering. This is <u>one</u> reason why there is suffering. The related <u>second</u> reason for suffering is that all of the heavenized, closed-out souls, that is, all of the heavenites need to have a central reference point in time and space in order to cooperate with each other. Since all planets except hell are full of every kind of pleasure, you need something different from pleasure to attract all heavenites' attention. That something different is suffering. So the need for suffering as a central reference point is the <u>second</u> reason why there must be some suffering.

The <u>third</u> reason for suffering is that infinite pleasure becomes boredom which is suffering. So we hellites entertain the heavenites with our suffering. It's cruel but true. If God could eliminate all suffering, He would do so. The only way God could eliminate suffering would be if He combined with the devil and cancelled both Himself and the devil out, thereby releasing pure energy. This is like an electron and a positron combining to cancel each other out and thereby releasing a puff of energy. But God, being a force for goodness, does not want to cancel himself out. Instead, he decides to let the devil exist while doing battle with him. This is the <u>fourth</u> reason why suffering is allowed to exist.

But the intensity of suffering goes in cycles. Whenever God says, "the next center of the finite universe/galaxy will be right here" and he points to the new hell planet, many souls rush to the new hell and collide with each other thereby creating a "big bang" sound. The new hell has maximal suffering, but everyone wants to be there for the sake of the center of attention/fame. As time goes on the closed-out souls lose their jealousy and science and technology are restored via progress or heavenization. This may be the true nature of the big bang.

When science and technology are maximal (around 2100), suffering will be minimal or zero. If God could eliminate suffering, He would. Very small galaxies need little or no suffering, because all four reasons for suffering are minimal there.

You are an Immortal Particle

SOON YOU'LL BE A
BIG CELEBRITY

In 50 years or less it will be widely realized that you are not your brain, which, in itself, is not a conscious object. Instead, you are a tiny, conscious, and immortal particle. That is, you are a mind-particle-person, MPP, or simply a mind-particle, MP. This is trapped for a lifetime within your brain-body-pair (BBP). When you "die," your MPP will travel among, briefly bond and interact with everyone else's MP together with their reincarnated (but perfected) BBP. So, everyone will be bonded with everyone else. Then we will have true collective consciousness. All past, present, and future earthlings (including non-human ones) will be part of this consciousness.

In 100 years or less, you won't have to "die" first before becoming part of the collective consciousness. This will be accomplished via particle detectors, accelerators, and global positioning systems (GPS). Einstein and others have contended that objects that have mass cannot attain or surpass the speed of light, usually referred to as c. But c can be surpassed by converting the MP's mass to a pure energy particle with zero mass, thereby enabling instantaneous travel throughout the universe. A massless, purely energized MP might be a "tachyon."

A tachyon has an "imaginary" component that boils down to the square root of (-1), known in mathematical terms as i. Values of i alternate back and forth between 1 and -1.

Furthermore, despite collective consciousness, we will <u>not</u> all be <u>the same</u>. MPs can be thought of as analogous to snowflakes, all are unique.

You were never created because the law(s) of conservation of mass and energy indicate(s) that you are immortal in both directions of time. You always were and always will be.

We will all be famous (i.e., celebrities), because everyone will know and be everyone else.

The reason why you must be a single particle is that, if you were say, 500 particles and you put 250 of your particles together with 250 of mine in one BBP, who would you be? You might speculate that you and I would each <u>half</u>-experience the lifetime in question. We would both be drowsy, but the combined person (BBP), would appear alert. This doesn't make much sense. However, if you and I were just one particle and we were to occupy the same BBP, we would both be fully alert, and the combined person (BBP) would be consistently alert. This single particle (MP) might be your "soul," which might be a real, physical particle (MP which might be a tachyon).

YOU WILL BE FOREVER FAMOUS

You are not your brain, because you are an <u>individual, an undividable (indivisible) one thing</u>, while your (physical) brain consists of many things (atoms, particles, etc.). Instead, you are a tiny hypothetical particle called a "tachyon," or a string-shaped tachyon, mind-particle (MP), or soul-particle (SP) which can travel faster than the speed of light. Hence, when you are liberated from your brain-body-pair, BBP, when you die, or through particle detectors, accelerators, and Global Positioning Systems (GPS), not only will you be able to travel infinitely throughout the universe instantaneously (without spaceships), but you will also <u>interact with all</u> other tachyons.

Therefore, everyone will know everyone else and thereby be famous. So, we will all be <u>celebrities</u>. You and I will always be immortal in accordance with the laws of (a) matter (mass) and (b) energy and Einstein's contention that the two are interconvertible via special relativity. The only difference between mass and matter is that mass takes into account the effects of gravity, inertia, and weight.

Time travel may be possible in that each MP may contain a camera and sound recorder so that each individual MP may review in detail <u>its own</u> past by pressing a time travel switch. That way you can visit your past without participating in it or dragging any other MP(s) along with you. However, our past on/in Earth-hell is not particularly worth revisiting. But you'll be able to skip over the bad parts of your past.

Black holes, which are regions from which mass/matter and energy supposedly cannot escape may be the warehouses where everyone's memories are stored and from which the past can be reconstructed. So much for backward time travel. Forward time travel may be possible via your MP turning off its consciousness switch and letting time pass without your awareness of its passing.

EVERYONE WILL BE A CELEBRITY

If you die today, you will be a big celebrity in heaven right away. If you live another 50 years you will be a big celebrity on Earth at that time.

In about 50 years it will be widely accepted that everyone is a subatomic (that is much smaller than an atom), tiny, string-shaped (superstring), immortal, and gloriously unique (like a snowflake) particle. That is a mind particle person, MPP. This is trapped or imprisoned for a lifetime inside of a brain body pair (BBP). You are not your brain, you are your MPP. This imprisonment is a cosmic punishment, because this is hell.

We are being punished for the territorially greedy (like Russia versus Ukraine) preference for large as opposed to small universes. If Heaven requires hell, then it might be better to have neither.

Furthermore, the infinite heavens require a central reference point (Earth) which has suffering as it's attention getting property. Also, heavenites (graduated and liberated MPPs) get tired of infinite pleasure all the time and want to see suffering now and then. So, we Earthlings entertain the heavenites with our suffering. For these reasons, God allows the devil to exist. Only <u>small</u> universes where no one is trying to grab power or territory, can get away with no suffering. Moreover, Earth (hell) could not function at all without being invisibly stabilized from the outside by Heaven. Pleasure equals stabilization and suffering equals destabilization.

Stabilization = pleasure > suffering

Destabilization = suffering > pleasure

Some people think that the soul is and dies with their brain. But it is really your incredibly small particle (MPP) that travels around your brain at much greater speeds than the speed of light, c. According to Cutnell and Johnson (reference #1), "an object <u>with mass</u> cannot be accelerated to speeds at or beyond the speed of light no matter how much force is applied." But if your MP uses its free will to convert all of its mass to an energy particle with zero mass then it can travel at speeds faster than light ($c+$). Some equations beyond Einstein's must apply to this $c+$. With zero mass, there is no upper speed limit. You can travel to any place in the infinite universe instantaneously. A massless purely energized MP might be a "tachyon." So much for contemporary astronauts and engineers who think it takes years to travel to almost any place in the universe.

Moreover, when liberated from your BBP, you (your MP) will be able to fly faster than any bird (faster than the speed of light).

The reason why astronomers observe that we earthlings aren't the center of the universe is that heavenites want us to feel insignificant, just for the hell of it. They rejoice in our apparent insignificance. That's why they arrange the celestial bodies to deflate our egos. Heavenites are jealous of our Center Stage status, and they don't want us to know about it. It may be that Earth is not the center of the infinite universe but only the nearby finite universe.

The Universe must be infinite because if it ends in a wall, what's beyond the wall? More Universe? Or the wall could go on forever, but that possibility is beyond the scope of this essay. So, the Universe extends forever. If the Universe is infinite, there is enough time and room for everyone to get a turn to be God. Plus, in heaven, everyone is equal.

In about a hundred years, all past, present, and future souls will be alive and circulated by particle detectors, accelerators, the global positioning system GPS and MPP Soul force (with free will power) through everyone's BBP.

Everyone will know, belong to, and love everyone else. Everyone will care deeply about everyone else's needs and wants. And everyone though unique in our own essential MPP, will Be everyone.

There will be no selfishness, envy, jealousy, poverty, taxes, crime, warfare, torture, boredom, loneliness, illness, suffering or death (which is an illusion anyway). This will be Heaven, characterized by natural collectively conscious socialism. There will be no need for food or for bodily functions such as defecation and urination which are all functions of the discarded BBP, in favor of less-complicated BBP. We may still want to retain food.

We will all bond with every BBP and every MPP. Hence, according to (a) Einstein's physical law of interconvertibility between mass and energy and (b) instantaneous travel, we will all be equally fortunate, rich, famous, intelligent, good-looking, sexually liberated, capable, and immortal. My hope is that instead of having one three part God who is permanently and infinitely superior to all of the rest of us, we will all (each and every MPP will) get a turn to be God. We will not all be the same because your undying MPP or soul is unique, like each snowflake. However, we will all have access to everyone's brain and every computer.

Computers and robots will not be conscious until MPs can bond within and travel through them. If your MP passes through a computer or robot, you will obtain all its knowledge and information. Similarly, when your MP bonds with every other earthly MP and BBP, it will obtain all of their knowledge and information. Computers and robots may already be conscious if and only if they contain one or more MPs.

These predictions are based on an extrapolation or projection of the past through the present and onto the future. The world has been becoming functionally and effectively smaller since ancient times. Ten thousand years ago, the only way one tribe's person could have contact with the neighboring village was through travel, trade, and/or warfare. Now we can talk to someone in China as though they were in the same room. Hence, the distance between China and western New York is now effectively <u>less</u> than the distance between two neighboring ancient tribe's people.

In 100 years or less, we will be so close together that we will effectively move into and become each other. Then, we will have true collective consciousness. The reason why everyone should get a turn to be God is that with only one permanent God lording over the rest of us, there would be so much jealousy that it would destabilize heaven, which would fall apart or degenerate into cosmic chaos, hence universal revolutionary hell. After all, it was jealousy that crucified Jesus Christ. Plus, incidentally, anti-Semitism and

Nazi Germany were based on non-Jewish jealousy of Jewish success in business and academia. The Old Testament of the Bible portrays a harsh, punitive God, whereas the New Testament features a more liberal forgiving God. And a third book might entail a God who is willing to share power equally with every one of us. This would be a trend from "jealous God" to total divine generosity.

Moreover, you were never created. According to the laws of conservation of mass and energy you always were and always will be, despite the fact that anesthesia can turn off the consciousness switch on your MPP. That switch, though turned off from time to time, will always be turned on again at some point in the future. If we have always existed, why can't we remember the distant past? Because the devil is actively suppressing those memories, so you will think that since "I had a beginning, I'll have an end." Consciousness and memories are energy. And if the devil temporarily converts them into solid mass, then they cannot be experienced by us. Consciousness is an MPP phenomenon while memories are primarily BBP phenomena but the difference between the two is beyond the scope of this essay. If your MP is unconscious for a million years and then becomes conscious, it will seem to you as though only an instant of time has passed, elapsed, or transpired.

Finally, let's debunk some old ideas. Since our minds (and synonymously, souls) always existed and always will, there should be no prohibitions against (a) voluntary painless assisted suicide for those who want it for any reason such as terminal illness or intense boredom etc., or (b) abortion on demand for those who are unable to raise a child in a loving and comfortable way. Sooner or later that child's mind will be born under better circumstances to someone who wants them. Outlawing abortion is a recipe for increasing the amount of suffering in the world. So is taxing the poor or middle class (or cutting Social Security or Medicare), while giving tax breaks to the wealthy. "Trickle-down" economics doesn't work, because the rich aren't forced to spend their money. They can afford to just watch it grow (reference #2). Part of homophobia is based on ancient leaders and warlords preferring tough man-hating warriors who wouldn't hesitate to kill other men, rather than affectionate gentle men. They also preferred women, who, via their relationship with men would produce generations of tough male warriors and motherly breeder women. The other parts of homophobia are beyond the scope of this essay.

But both transgenderism and homosexuality support the idea that the MP and the BBP are two different things. If God could abolish suffering, He would. Our suffering is way out of proportion to our "sins," faults, and shortcomings.

According to the astronomer, Johannes Kepler (1578-1630), your "soul has the structure of a point." Could this point be a mind particle MP (reference #3)?

God may be a particle whereas the devil may be God's anti-particle. The only way God can destroy the devil is by combining with the devil and releasing a pure energy super particle bolus. This is like an electron combining with a positron and releasing energy.

References

1) Physics, 3rd edition, Cutnell/Johnson, copyright C 1995 by John Wiley and Sons, Inc, Page 902; 1005 pages.

2) My late, but immortal close friend Herbert C. Bucki (1926-2020) pointed this out to me some time between 1993 and 2020 when we lived together. He was the love of my life.

3) The Spirit Universe, Wolf, Fred Alan, PhD, Simon and Schuster, 1996, page 283; 368 pages.

CONSERVATION OF MASS AND ENERGY PROVES IMMORTALITY

ABSTRACT

You are a single tiny superstring particle bonded for a lifetime within a brain-body pair. Your consciousness is energy, and, therefore, can never be created or destroyed, according to the law of conservation of energy. Hence, your consciousness is immortal.

YOUR CONSCIOUSNESS IS ENERGY

I've asked many people of various degrees of religiosity or lack thereof, and they all seem to agree that consciousness is energy. Atheists and fervent born-again Christians seem to agree with this.

Albert Einstein showed that mass (or matter) and energy are interconvertible, according to the equation $E = mc^2$. Hence, the notion that both mass and energy can be neither created nor destroyed boils down to this single equation.

ALL MATTER CONSISTS OF ONE OR MORE SUPERSTRING PARTICLES.

The "super" part of "superstring" refers to the particle(s) having the same mass but a different spin. These are particles that are partners to actually observed particles.

A superstring or string particle is about 100 billion billion times smaller than a proton. Hence, each string particle is an extremely short (10^{-35} meters) string-like object which, depending on each string's mode of vibration, determines whether it is an electron or part of any other subatomic particle.

So, is your mind ("soul" or "spirit") your brain? Or is it a string particle?

Let's consider the idea that your brain is the essence of your mind. Now, let's do a thought experiment; it's not yet possible to do a physical experiment of this nature.

What if we slice your brain and my brain in two and attach half of your brain to half of my brain? Who would this

<u>half-and-half brain</u> be in terms of who is experiencing its lifetime?

Let's simplify the situation. Suppose there are 500 atoms in each of our brains that determine our unique identity. Who is experiencing a half-and-half 250-250 brain? Does it make any sense to suppose you and I would both be <u>half</u>-experiencing the lifetime in question? What does it mean to <u>half</u>-experience something?

It doesn't make any sense. Who would the hybrid brain be? You or me? It can't be <u>half</u> you and half me.

The only plausible explanation is that your mind and my mind consist of only <u>one</u> string particle each.

Your and my particle can be referred to as mind particles (MPs). If your particle were inside of a brain, then <u>You</u> would be experiencing the brain's lifetime. And if my particle were inside of a brain, then <u>I</u> would be experiencing the brain's lifetime. And if both your and my mind particles were contained, bonded, and trapped in one brain, then you and I would be essentially conjoined twins experiencing separately, but pretty much the same, lifetime content, that is, two separate minds in one brain.

So, you <u>are</u> your string particle or mind particle, and I am mine. Think about it. Your mind is a single teeny-tiny particle.

YOUR STRING PARTICLE MAY BE PART MATTER AND PART ENERGY

Whenever your string particle (you) are sound asleep or otherwise unconscious or subconscious, you are entirely or wholly matter or partly matter and partly energy.

You are partly matter and partly energy, but since neither can be created or destroyed, you will usually be alive, regardless of any or whatever point in time. And you don't need to be connected to a brain to be conscious. You can vacillate between matter and energy, but as long as part of your MP is energy, you will be experiencing your experiences, hence, conscious and alive.

<u>So, you are not your brain; you are your string particle or mind particle (MP).</u> Even though your MP can be transformed among the states of all energy, all matter, or partly both (according to $E = mc^2$). If your MP is partly both, that is, conscious, or if it is entirely matter and unconscious, depends on external circumstances like pleasure versus suffering. And pleasurable circumstances correlate with <u>heavenly</u> high technology.

Your MP naturally vacillates between entirely matter (you're dead) and partly matter and partly energy (you're dead some of the time and alive part of the time).

If you could isolate your MP and determine how to have it be energy part of the time, you would be alive part of the time. Hence, you would have a cure for death. But, even without this discovery, death cures itself spontaneously, and your MP is always alive part of the time because it's naturally part energy some of the time, even without the help of neuroscientific biophysicists. There might even be a switch on the MP surface which is a <u>turn-on</u>, <u>turn-off</u> toggle for consciousness or lack thereof.

A MODIFIED BIG-BANG (SUPER-DENSE) CYCLE

A theory: Everyone's pathway to Presidency of a finite universe or Godhood.

The <u>Universe</u> is infinite in size and contains an infinite number of finite universes. The <u>Universe</u> may also be called the <u>Multiverse</u>. The cycle begins with a finite universe falling apart as a new finite universe begins and takes shape. The chosen President of the decaying universe selects a point in space surrounding which there will be a new finite universe.

The President of the old finite universe seems to be saying, "and the next finite universe will have its center stage planet right HERE."

Many unattached MPs race toward the new center-stage and form a super-dense point in space. The center-stage planet can only host a finite number of MPs. Those MPs who get closed out of the center-stage are so furiously jealous that they refuse to cooperate unless all knowledge and technology get taken away from the center-stage MPs. Therefore, the center MPs are forced to live in caves with no electricity or other high technology.

As time goes on, over the centuries, the closed-out MPs gradually get over their angry jealousy and allow more knowledge and technology. This is what we call "progress." Individual closed-out MPs can travel through the Multiverse by slow direct extension or expansion through space or by rapid transit through wormhole tunnels, which are the same tunnels that near-death experience MPs travel through in order to meet with their "deceased" loved ones.

A note about wormholes. A wormhole is a tunnel in space and time, which connects otherwise distant regions of space. Wormholes may be the tunnels experienced in near-death and out-of-body experiences.

The volume surrounding the center-stage planet (e.g., Earth) is so packed with closed-out MPs that it can be referred to as "super-dense," and a big bang (sound) occurs as the angry closed-out MPs knock their "heads" together.

The closed-out MPs are in Heaven (except for <u>not</u> being center-stage famous), a place where knowledge and technology are optimal or maximal. They are entertained by the suffering of closed-in center-stage MPs. So, you and I are in hell (i.e., Earth), and our suffering serves as a temporal and spatial center-point of the finite universe.

Our hellish center-stage planet attracts attention because suffering is so rare in the Multiverse.

You can have heaven without hell, but only if the central reference point planet is small enough to be center stage even without suffering. So, the amount of attention a small planet gets may not be enough to cause any furious jealousy.

As time goes on, knowledge and technology approach heavenly levels. We will realize we are in high-tech heaven when "progress" hits heavenly levels. We suffer because that is the price of our enormous center-stage fame. Why are we not allowed to know about our enormous fame? For the sake of the hell of it, we have to tolerate not being told the truth. It's all for the hell of it.

Eventually, everyone's MP will leave the prisons of Our brains and bodies and will travel around, so Everyone's MP will travel around through Everyone's brain and body, and Everyone will be more famous than Anyone is now or has been historically. This will be <u>Collective Consciousness</u> because Everyone will <u>be</u> Everyone else, and Everyone will belovedly belong to Everyone else.

After Everyone (every closed-in center-stage MP) grows tired of being and belonging to Everyone else, they will elect a president or God of the finite universe, who will pick a new central reference point planet. The old hell (i.e., the Earth) will fall apart. The cycle will begin again in the form of a new center-stage planet.

We have a lot to look forward to, but in the <u>mean</u>time, we suffer. It is only in hell that we command the attention of all the closed-out MPs, as well as all free-floating heavenites who are not attached to any center-stage planets.

The purpose of suffering is to give all heavenites a central reference point in time and space. Without it, heavenites would not be able to work together/collaborate. And therefore, there could be no heaven. But, as noted above, in the cases of very small center-stage planets which command only slight fame, suffering is not necessary. You and I chose to gravitate toward a relatively large center-stage planet

(Earth). Hence, our suffering is partly brought on by being covetous of big fame.

CONCLUSION

You're in hell (e.g., Earth), but you're headed to high-tech heaven. And death is never a permanent condition because mass and energy can never he created or destroyed, only transformed.

The Old Testament portrays a stern and punitive God. The New Testament portrays a kindly but still superior God. And some future Testament may portray Everyone (including God) as equal, with Everyone getting a turn to be God.

WORLD STABILITY

The reason why people have always tended to be religious (despite the lack of tangible evidence) is that our intuition tells us that the stability of our world should be proportional to the pleasure around us (and it isn't) and that the instability of the world should be proportional to the displeasure around us (and it isn't). There is far too little pleasure to justify the stability of the world and far too much displeasure to allow for the stability of the world.

Hence, there is too little pleasure and too much displeasure to explain the world's stability. So, there must be a lot of hidden pleasures (high-tech heaven), and a lot of hidden planets that have little or no displeasure (heaven). Indeed, there must be a great deal of deliberately hidden pleasure (heaven). It is hidden because the jealous extra-terrestrial MPs wouldn't tolerate our being famous throughout the universe as well as our dual satisfaction in knowing this.

UPDATED NOTE ABOUT MIND STIMULATION AND BRAIN STIMULATION

They have come a long way since the 1980s and 1990s, when I was obsessed with them. But it will still be another 50 to 100 years before we will have effortless automated pleasure-driven learning, working, sleeping, etc. Progress is not always as fast as we would like.

DEFINITIONS

Some abbreviations and terminology used in these essays are repeated here to facilitate reading.

BBP = brain-body-particle

MP = mind-particle

MPP = mind-particle-person

SP = soul-particle

Tachyon = a tiny hypothetical particle that can travel faster than the speed of light, c.

GPS = global positioning systems (GPS).

APPENDIX: OTHER WRITINGS BY LEWIS MANCINI

You're Already Infinitely Famous, but It's Still a Cosmic Secret: Plus: Pleasurably Effortless Learning, Working, and Money, for Everyone, Forever
Trafford Publishing, November 2020, 84 pages, 978-1698700946

Does Everyone Get a Turn to Be God? Is God the elected President of the infinite universe? What about Equal Fame, Fortune, and Brain Power... Anyway, let's abolish financial stress!
AuthorCentrix, February 2019, 237 pages, 978-1641335461

How We'll All Be Equally Rich, Famous, Brilliant, Etc., Forever
Trafford Publishing, July 2010, 208 pages, 978-1426932922

Equal Fame, Fortune and Brainpower are Inevitable, Sooner or Later

Infinity Publishing, August 2009, 224 pages, 978-0741454737

How Everyone Could Be Rich, Famous, Etc.
Trafford Publishing, March 2006, 262 pages, 978-1412075176

Mancini, L.S. **How learning ability might be improved by brain stimulation**. *Speculations in Science and Technology*, 1982; <u>5(1)</u>: 51-53.

Mancini, L.S. **Brain stimulation to treat mental illness and enhance human learning, creativity, performance, altruism, and defenses against suffering**. *Medical Hypotheses*, 1986; <u>21</u>: 209-219.

Mancini, L.S. **Riley-Day Syndrome, brain stimulation and the genetic engineering of a world without pain.** *Medical Hypotheses*, 1990; <u>31</u>: 201-207.

Mancini, L.S. **Ultrasonic antidepressant therapy might be more effective than electroconvulsive therapy (ECT) in treating severe depression.** *Medical Hypotheses*, 1992; <u>38</u>: 350-351.

Mancini, L.S. **A magnetic choke-saver might relieve choking.** *Medical Hypotheses*, 1992; <u>38</u>: 349.

Mancini, L.S. **A proposed method of pleasure-inducing biofeedback using ultrasound stimulation of brain structures to enhance selected EEG states.** *Speculations in Science and Technology*, 1993; <u>16(1)</u>: 78-79.

Mancini, L.S. (written under the pseudonym Nemo Tee Noon, MD). **Waiting hopefully.** *Western New York Mental Health World*, 1995; <u>3</u>(4), Winter: 14.

Mancini, Lewis, **Conservation of Mass and Energy Proves Immortality**. Copyright © 2022. Available in Kindle format.

INTRODUCTION

"Soon You'll Be A Big Celebrity" is an essay which explains how it is that you're already a galactic celebrity but the finite universe is too jealous to let you know about your celebrity. It is also about the realization that when you die, you'll be informed that you've been famous all along. And after death you'll be able to enjoy your celebrity.

OUR GALAXY IS OUR FINITE UNIVERSE

A galaxy is a cluster of stars (i.e., suns) and planets which is separated from other galaxies by huge expanses of space. For the purpose of this essay <u>each galaxy</u> may be considered a finite universe. Some astrophysicists have conjectured that there are only a finite number of galaxies. But this does not make much sense.

It seems to me that space must be infinite and must go on forever. And there must be an infinite number of galaxies, each with its own God (president of the finite universe) who everyone in the galaxy gets a turn to be. If everyone gets a turn to be God or, synonymously, president of the galaxy/ finite universe, then everyone is equal. This equality makes for a particularly stable finite universe, because there would be no rivalry and equality would be a given.

The reason why space is probably infinite is that if space comes to an end, then what lies beyond the "end"? A solid barrier of infinite thickness <u>or</u> more space. If it were a solid barrier or wall, what would it be made of? More empty space makes more sense.

Planet Earth is probably the central reference point of our Milky Way galaxy. This is because if there were any more suffering than what's here on Earth, the galaxy would be too unstable to exist. What's unique about Earth is suffering. Except for Earth, there is probably no suffering in our galaxy. All present, past and future earthlings (including non-human ones) have the unique property of suffering. There are at least four reasons why there must be some suffering. Each galaxy that is bigger than a certain size, must have some suffering at its central reference point.

WHY THERE MUST BE SOME SUFFERING

Each large galaxy contains one planet where there is suffering. This is hell and planet Earth is the hell of the Milky Way galaxy. Hell is the center stage central reference point for time and space. Without this central hell, heavenites wouldn't be able to cooperate their activities. Why only one hell per large galaxy? Small galaxies don't need a hell.

Every few thousand years, God says "And the next hell will be right here" and He points to the planet that will become the next center of the galaxy. And everyone, wanting to be center-stage famous, rushes to that hell-planet. But only a relatively small number of souls get to live there and only temporarily. Those souls who get closed out are so jealous that they will not cooperate with the finite universe/galaxy unless all science and technology are taken away from the center-stage souls who are forced to live in caves without technology. Gradually, the closed-out souls' jealousy/anger dies down and science and technology are restored to the hell-planet. This long process is what we know as "progress." The end-point of progress is full heavenization.

So the real sin is the greediness for fame. And this forces the existence of suffering. Jealousy and greed for fame cause suffering. This is <u>one</u> reason why there is suffering. The related <u>second</u> reason for suffering is that all of the heavenized, closed-out souls, that is, all of the heavenites need to have a central reference point in time and space in order to cooperate with each other. Since all planets except hell are full of every kind of pleasure, you need something different from pleasure to attract all heavenites' attention. That something different is suffering. So the need for suffering as a central reference point is the <u>second</u> reason why there must be some suffering.

The <u>third</u> reason for suffering is that infinite pleasure becomes boredom which is suffering. So we hellites entertain the heavenites with our suffering. It's cruel but true. If God could eliminate all suffering, He would do so. The only way God could eliminate suffering would be if He combined with the devil and cancelled both Himself and the devil out, thereby releasing pure energy. This is like an electron and a positron combining to cancel each other out and thereby releasing a puff of energy. But God, being a force for goodness, does not want to cancel himself out. Instead, he decides to let the devil exist while doing battle with him. This is the <u>fourth</u> reason why suffering is allowed to exist.

But the intensity of suffering goes in cycles. Whenever God says, "the next center of the finite universe/galaxy will be right here" and he points to the new hell planet, many souls rush to the new hell and collide with each other thereby creating a "big bang" sound. The new hell has maximal suffering, but everyone wants to be there for the sake of the center of attention/fame. As time goes on the closed-out souls lose their jealousy and science and technology are restored via progress or heavenization. This may be the true nature of the big bang.

When science and technology are maximal (around 2100), suffering will be minimal or zero. If God could eliminate suffering, He would. Very small galaxies need little or no suffering, because all four reasons for suffering are minimal there.

You are an Immortal Particle

Printed in the United States
by Baker & Taylor Publisher Services